Walking

Rodriquez McGruder

United States of America

Published by Shooting Stars Publishing House 2024

Dedication

To everyone that desires a closer relationship with God. It's time to begin your new walk today.

Contents

Introduction

In the relentless hustle and bustle of modern life, where every moment seems consumed by the demands of work, family, and technology, it's all too easy for spirituality to become lost in the shuffle. Yet, even amidst the cacophony of daily existence, there exists a tranquil, almost clandestine path waiting to be discovered—a path that leads us away from the frenetic pace of the world and towards a deeper connection with our Creator. "Walking with God" isn't merely another addition to the countless devotional offerings available today; rather, it stands as a poignant and compelling invitation—an invitation to embark on a profoundly modern journey of faith, one that transcends the noise and distractions of our time.

Within the pages of this devotional, we won't merely skim the surface of spirituality; instead, we'll embark on an immersive exploration, delving deep into the sacred texts and timeless wisdom that have guided countless seekers throughout the ages. Through thoughtful reflections, poignant anecdotes, and insightful commentary, we'll navigate the complexities of modern life while remaining rooted in the eternal truths of faith. We'll uncover the relevance of scripture in our contemporary context, discovering how its timeless principles can illuminate our path and offer solace in times of uncertainty.

Moreover, "Walking with God" isn't just about solitary introspection; it's about community and connection—a shared journey undertaken alongside fellow travelers on the road of faith. As we journey together, we'll share in each other's joys and struggles, offering support, encouragement, and companionship along the way. Through the power of storytelling, we'll find common ground, recognizing our shared humanity and the universal truths that bind us together. And through the practice of prayer, we'll forge a direct line of communication with the Divine, fostering a sense of intimacy and closeness that transcends time and space.

In essence, "Walking with God" is an invitation to step off the treadmill of busyness and enter into a sacred space of reflection, renewal, and spiritual growth. It's an opportunity to slow down, to pause, and to reconnect with that which is most essential and enduring in life. So, as we embark on this journey together, may we open our hearts, minds, and spirits to the transformative power of faith, trusting that in walking with God, we'll find the strength, guidance, and sustenance we need to navigate the complexities of the modern world.

Chapter 1:
Surrendering to Divine Guidance

In the fast-paced world we live in, the desire for control is ingrained within us. We strive to plan every detail of our lives, clinging tightly to the illusion of certainty. However, as we journey deeper into our spiritual walk, we encounter a profound truth: true freedom lies in surrendering control to a higher power.

In this chapter, we embark on a journey of relinquishing our grip on the reins and entrusting our lives to the divine guidance of God. Through relatable anecdotes and practical exercises, we delve into the liberating act of letting go and letting God. We confront our innate need for control, recognizing the limitations of our human understanding, and embrace the profound truth that God's plan far surpasses our own.

Drawing inspiration from contemporary figures and real-life experiences, we are reminded of the transformative power of surrender. We hear stories of individuals who, in moments of desperation or uncertainty, released their fears and doubts into the hands of God, only to discover a peace that surpasses all understanding. From the single parent struggling to make ends meet to the corporate executive facing a crossroads in their career, each narrative serves as a testament to the profound freedom that comes from surrendering to divine guidance.

Through practical exercises and reflection prompts, readers are invited to confront their own struggles with control and surrender. We explore the fears and insecurities that often hold us back from relinquishing control, and we challenge ourselves to trust in God's plan for our lives, even when it diverges from our own expectations. As we release our grip on the illusion of control, we open ourselves up to a deeper sense of purpose and fulfillment, allowing God to lead us on a journey of discovery and transformation.

Ultimately, this chapter serves as a gentle reminder that true freedom is found not in the pursuit of control, but in the surrender to divine guidance. As we embrace the liberating truth that God's plan far exceeds our own, we step into a life of greater peace, joy, and fulfillment, trusting that in letting go, we find our truest selves in the loving embrace of our God.

Chapter 2:
Putting Faith in the Journey

In the mosaic of modern life, trust serves as the glue that connects us to our Divine Creator. It's the unshakeable belief that even amidst life's toughest trials, God's promises remain rock-solid. In this chapter, we set off on a contemporary voyage of faith, exploring the game-changing power of trust in God's grand design.

Through tales of resilience and optimism, we witness firsthand the life-altering influence of trust, even in the face of daunting challenges. From timeless biblical narratives to the real-world experiences of everyday heroes, we encounter stories of triumph over adversity that underscore the unwavering reliability of God. Whether it's the account of a young entrepreneur weathering setbacks before achieving success or the inspiring journey of a refugee finding hope against all odds, each tale serves as a beacon of hope, lighting up the path of trust in God's promises.

In the whirlwind of life's uncertainties, we're called to lean into our faith and trust in God's boundless love and provision.

Through practical reflections and actionable advice, readers are encouraged to deepen their trust in God's blueprint, even when the path ahead seems murky. We confront our doubts and anxieties head-on, recognizing the frailty of our human understanding, and choose to anchor our faith in the enduring character of God.

Furthermore, we come to understand that trust isn't merely a passive nod to fate, but an active surrender to God's guidance in our lives. Through mindfulness practices and intentional prayer, we cultivate an attitude of openness and receptivity, allowing God to chart our course and mold our destinies. As we relinquish our need for control and embrace the mystery of God's ways, we discover solace in the knowledge that His plans for us are nothing short of extraordinary, even if they veer off from our preconceived notions.

Ultimately, this chapter serves as a testament to the life-changing potential of trust in God's promises. As we navigate the rollercoaster ride of modern existence, may we anchor our faith in His unwavering love, knowing that by trusting in the journey, we find resilience, optimism, and the comforting assurance of His presence walking alongside us.

Chapter 3:
Embracing the Power of Thankfulness

In a world that often seems fixated on what's lacking rather than what's present, gratitude emerges as a potent force in our spiritual quest. It's the secret ingredient that transforms our perspective, infusing each moment with newfound joy and appreciation. In this chapter, we embark on a journey of discovery, exploring the transformative power of gratitude and its profound impact on our spiritual well-being.

Scripture reminds us time and again of the importance of gratitude in our lives. In the book of Psalms, we find the psalmist declaring, "Give thanks to the Lord, for he is good; his love endures forever" (Psalm 107:1, NIV). Similarly, in his letter to the Philippians, the apostle Paul encourages believers to "Rejoice in the Lord always. I will say it again: Rejoice!" (Philippians 4:4, NIV). These verses serve as poignant reminders of the transformative power of gratitude in shifting our focus from life's challenges to the blessings that abound.

In today's fast-paced world, where distractions abound and negativity often reigns supreme, cultivating an attitude of gratitude can seem like a daunting task. However, through modern practices like journaling and mindfulness, we can train our minds to recognize and appreciate the blessings that surround us. By intentionally pausing to reflect on the moments of beauty, joy, and abundance in our lives, we begin to cultivate a heart of gratitude that transcends circumstances.

Moreover, the practice of thankfulness not only enhances our personal well-being but also deepens our connection with the Divine. As we express gratitude for the blessings bestowed upon us, we acknowledge God's goodness and faithfulness in our lives. The apostle Paul reminds us of this truth in his letter to the Thessalonians, saying, "Give thanks in all circumstances; for this is God's will for you in Christ Jesus" (1 Thessalonians 5:18, NIV). By aligning our hearts with God's will through the practice of thankfulness, we open ourselves up to a deeper sense of fulfillment and joy.

Gratitude isn't just a fleeting emotion; it's a way of life—a conscious choice to focus on the blessings rather than the burdens, the joys rather than the sorrows. As we journey through life with hearts full of gratitude, may we experience the transformative power of thankfulness in deepening our connection with God and finding true fulfillment in every moment.

Chapter 4:
Finding Liberation Through Forgiveness

Forgiveness stands as a cornerstone of our faith journey, a profound act that releases us from the chains of bitterness and resentment. In this chapter, we embark on a deep dive into the transformative power of forgiveness and its pivotal role in healing fractured relationships and fostering inner peace.

Scripture offers us timeless wisdom on the subject of forgiveness, urging us to emulate the boundless grace and mercy of our Creator. In the Gospel of Matthew, Jesus teaches his disciples to pray, saying, "Forgive us our debts, as we also have forgiven our debtors" (Matthew 6:12, NIV). Similarly, in his letter to the Colossians, the apostle Paul admonishes believers to "Bear with each other and forgive one another if any of you has a grievance against someone. Forgive as the Lord forgave you" (Colossians 3:13, NIV). These verses underscore the transformative power of forgiveness in our lives, both in our relationships with others and with God.

Yet, despite its importance, forgiveness is often one of the most challenging aspects of our faith journey. In the face of betrayal, hurt, and injustice, extending grace to those who have wronged us can feel like an insurmountable task. However, through relatable stories and practical advice, we discover that forgiveness is not just a gift we offer to others; it's a pathway to freedom and restoration in our own lives.

We explore the profound impact of forgiveness on our mental, emotional, and spiritual well-being, as well as its transformative effect on our relationships. Through the power of forgiveness, we release the burden of resentment and anger that weighs us down, allowing us to experience true liberation and inner peace. Just as Joseph forgave his brothers for their betrayal and Jesus extended forgiveness to those who crucified him, we learn to let go of past hurts and embrace the healing power of grace.

Moreover, we come to understand that forgiveness is not a one-time event but a continual process—a journey of letting go and choosing to live free from the shackles of unforgiveness. Through practical exercises and reflection prompts, readers are empowered to confront their own struggles with forgiveness and take steps toward healing and reconciliation. By embracing forgiveness as a lifestyle, we open ourselves up to a deeper experience of love, compassion, and restoration in our relationships with others and with God.

In conclusion, forgiveness isn't just a noble ideal; it's a transformative practice that leads to freedom and wholeness. As we journey through life with hearts open to forgiveness, may we experience the liberating power of grace in our relationships and find true peace in the embrace of God's boundless love.

Chapter 5:
Elevating Your Connection Through Prayer

In the hustle and bustle of modern life, amidst the clamor of notifications and distractions, prayer emerges as our lifeline to the divine—a sacred conversation that nourishes and strengthens our connection with God. In this chapter, we embark on a journey of exploration, delving into the myriad ways in which modern prayer practices can enrich and deepen our relationship with the Divine.

Scripture reminds us time and again of the importance of prayer in our spiritual lives. In the Gospel of Matthew, Jesus invites his disciples to "Ask and it will be given to you; seek and you will find; knock and the door will be opened to you" (Matthew 7:7, NIV). Similarly, in his letter to the Philippians, the apostle Paul encourages believers to "Do not be anxious about anything, but in every situation, by prayer and petition, with thanksgiving, present your requests to God" (Philippians 4:6, NIV). These verses underscore the transformative power of prayer in deepening our connection with God and experiencing His presence in our lives.

In today's technologically-driven world, the landscape of prayer has evolved, offering us a myriad of tools and resources to enhance our spiritual practice. From prayer apps that provide daily prompts and guided meditations to online communities that foster prayerful support and accountability, we have access to a wealth of modern prayer practices that can enrich our spiritual journey.

Through practical guidance and real-life examples, readers learn how to incorporate these modern prayer practices into their daily lives. Whether it's setting aside dedicated time for prayer each day, utilizing prayer apps to stay connected to God throughout the day, or participating in virtual prayer groups and communities, we discover practical ways to make prayer a priority in our lives.

Moreover, we come to understand that prayer is not merely a monologue, but a dialogue—a two-way conversation with God in which we both speak and listen. Through practices like journaling and contemplative prayer, we create space for God to speak to us, guiding us, and revealing His will for our lives.

Ultimately, this chapter serves as a reminder that prayer is not just a religious ritual, but a powerful tool for deepening our relationship with God and experiencing His presence in our daily lives. As we embrace modern prayer practices and make prayer a priority, may we cultivate a deeper sense of intimacy with the Divine, knowing that in His presence, we find strength, comfort, and guidance for the journey ahead.

Chapter 6:
Empowering Change Agents for a Modern World

In the age of unprecedented connectivity and rapid globalization, the call to action for followers of Christ resonates louder than ever. As we navigate the complexities of the modern world, we're reminded of our divine mandate to be agents of transformation, spreading God's love and compassion to all corners of society. In this final chapter, we embark on a journey of discovery, exploring the profound significance of serving others and making a positive impact in the world around us.

Scripture offers us a timeless blueprint for living out our faith in action. In the Gospel of Matthew, Jesus declares, "Truly I tell you, whatever you did for one of the least of these brothers and sisters of mine, you did for me" (Matthew 25:40, NIV). Similarly, in the letter of James, we're reminded that "faith by itself, if it is not accompanied by action, is dead" (James 2:17, NIV). These verses underscore the imperative of putting our faith into practice, demonstrating God's love through tangible acts of service and compassion.

In today's interconnected world, the opportunities to make a difference are endless. Through stories of compassion and activism, we witness the transformative power of individuals who have embraced their unique calling and made a tangible impact in their communities. From the tireless efforts of volunteers feeding the hungry and sheltering the homeless to the advocacy work of activists fighting for justice and equality, each narrative serves as a testament to the profound change that can occur when we channel God's love into action.

Moreover, we discover that making a difference in the modern world isn't just about grand gestures or heroic acts—it's about showing kindness and compassion in our everyday interactions. Whether it's lending a listening ear to a friend in need, extending a helping hand to a stranger, or speaking up for those who cannot advocate for themselves, we all have the power to make a positive impact in the lives of others.

Through practical guidance and reflection prompts, readers are empowered to discern their unique gifts and talents and identify opportunities for service in their own communities. Whether it's volunteering at a local charity, participating in a community clean-up initiative, or advocating for social justice causes, we discover that each of us has a vital role to play in building a better world.

Ultimately, this chapter serves as a rallying cry for believers to rise up and be the change they wish to see in the world. As we embrace our calling to serve others and spread God's love in the modern world, may we be inspired by the words of the apostle Paul, who reminds us that "we are God's handiwork, created in Christ Jesus to do good works, which God prepared in advance for us to do" (Ephesians 2:10, NIV). By answering this divine call to action, we become instruments of God's love and agents of transformation in a world hungry for hope and healing.

Chapter 7:
Embodying Christ's Love in Action

As we journey through life, we are called to embody the love and compassion of our merciful Savior, Jesus Christ. His life and teachings serve as a profound example of selfless love, urging us to extend grace and mercy to all whom we encounter. In this chapter, we delve into the transformative power of Christ's love and explore how we can emulate His example in our daily lives.

Scripture reminds us of the central importance of love in the Christian faith. In the Gospel of John, Jesus commands His disciples, saying, "A new command I give you: Love one another. As I have loved you, so you must love one another" (John 13:34, NIV). Similarly, in his first letter, the apostle John writes, "Dear friends, let us love one another, for love comes from God. Everyone who loves has been born of God and knows God" (1 John 4:7, NIV). These verses emphasize the foundational role of love in the Christian life and challenge us to mirror Christ's love in our relationships with others.

One of the hallmarks of Christ's love is His boundless compassion for the marginalized and the suffering. Throughout His ministry, Jesus demonstrated a profound empathy for those in need, healing the sick, comforting the brokenhearted, and ministering to the outcasts of society. As followers of Christ, we are called to emulate His example by opening our hearts to the needs of those around us and extending a helping hand to those who are hurting.

Moreover, Christ's love is characterized by humility and selflessness. In his letter to the Philippians, the apostle Paul exhorts believers to "Do nothing out of selfish ambition or vain conceit. Rather, in humility value others above yourselves, not looking to your own interests but each of you to the interests of the others" (Philippians 2:3-4, NIV). This admonition challenges us to set aside our own desires and preferences in order to prioritize the well-being of others, embodying the sacrificial love of Christ in our interactions.

As we seek to embody Christ's love in our lives, let us heed the words of the apostle Paul, who writes, "And over all these virtues put on love, which binds them all together in perfect unity"

(Colossians 3:14, NIV). May we strive to love others as Christ has loved us, with a love that knows no bounds and extends grace and mercy to all. And may our lives be a testament to the transformative power of Christ's love, shining brightly in a world in need of His healing touch. Amen.

Chapter 8:
The Power of Men and Women Walking Together with God

In a world often marked by division and discord, the image of men and women walking together with God stands as a powerful testament to the unity and harmony that can be achieved through shared faith and mutual respect. In this chapter, we explore the transformative power of collaboration between genders in the pursuit of a deeper relationship with the Divine.

Scripture affirms the equality and dignity of men and women as co-heirs in the Kingdom of God. In the book of Genesis, we read that God created humanity in His image, both male and female, declaring them to be equally valuable and worthy of honor (Genesis 1:27). Throughout the New Testament, we see Jesus breaking cultural norms by engaging with women as equals, affirming their worth and inviting them to participate fully in His ministry.

The power of men and women walking together with God lies in the unique perspectives, gifts, and strengths that each gender brings to the table. In his letter to the Corinthians, the apostle Paul writes, "There is neither Jew nor Greek, slave nor free, male nor female, for you are all one in Christ Jesus" (Galatians 3:28, NIV). This verse reminds us that in Christ, there is no distinction based on gender or social status—we are all united in our shared identity as beloved children of God.

When men and women come together in partnership and collaboration, they can more fully reflect the image of God and embody His love and grace in the world. In the book of Ecclesiastes, we read that "Two are better than one, because they have a good return for their labor: If either of them falls down, one can help the other up. But pity anyone who falls and has no one to help them up" (Ecclesiastes 4:9-10, NIV). This passage highlights the strength and support that can be found in companionship and collaboration, as well as the importance of walking together in unity and solidarity.

Moreover, the power of men and women walking together with God is evident in the diversity of perspectives and experiences that they bring to their shared journey of faith. Just as the body is made up of many parts, each with its own unique function, so too the Body of Christ is enriched and strengthened by the contributions of both men and women (1 Corinthians 12:12-27). When we come together in humility and mutual respect, recognizing and celebrating the gifts and talents of each individual, we create a more vibrant and inclusive community that reflects the diversity and beauty of God's creation.

The power of men and women walking together with God lies in the unity, strength, and diversity that they bring to their shared journey of faith. As we embrace our common identity as beloved children of God and seek to honor and affirm one another in our unique gifts and callings, may we experience the transformative power of collaboration and partnership in the pursuit of a deeper relationship with the Divine. And may our lives be a testimony to the boundless love and grace of our Creator, shining brightly in a world in need of healing and reconciliation.

Chapter 9:
Walking in Integrity in Our Relationship with God

Integrity forms the bedrock of our relationship with God, serving as the cornerstone of authentic faith and unwavering devotion. In this chapter, we explore the transformative power of walking in integrity in our journey with the Divine, grounded in the truth of God's Word and guided by His Spirit.

Scripture emphasizes the importance of integrity in our relationship with God. In the book of Proverbs, we read, "The integrity of the upright guides them, but the unfaithful are destroyed by their duplicity" (Proverbs 11:3, NIV). This verse highlights the pivotal role that integrity plays in guiding our decisions and actions, leading us along the path of righteousness and wisdom.

Walking in integrity means living in alignment with God's truth and moral principles, even when no one is watching. It involves honesty, transparency, and consistency in our words and deeds, reflecting the character of our Heavenly Father. In the Gospel of Matthew, Jesus instructs His disciples, saying, "Let your 'Yes' be yes, and your 'No,' no. Anything more comes from the evil one" (Matthew 5:37, NIV). This admonition challenges us to speak and act with integrity, honoring our commitments and remaining steadfast in our convictions.

Moreover, walking in integrity requires humility and accountability before God. In the book of Psalms, King David prays, "Test me, Lord, and try me, examine my heart and my mind; for I have always been mindful of your unfailing love and have lived in reliance on your faithfulness" (Psalm 26:2-3, NIV). This prayer reflects David's desire for God to examine his innermost thoughts and motives, acknowledging his dependence on God's grace and mercy to walk in integrity.

The power of walking in integrity in our relationship with God lies in the transformative impact it has on our character and witness. When we strive to live with integrity, we become beacons of light and truth in a world marked by deception and moral relativism. In his letter to the Ephesians, the apostle Paul exhorts believers to "Live as children of light...and find out what pleases the Lord"

(Ephesians 5:8,10, NIV). This call to holy living challenges us to shine with the radiance of God's truth and righteousness, bearing witness to His transformative power in our lives.

Walking in integrity in our relationship with God is not just a moral obligation—it's a sacred privilege and calling. As we align our hearts and minds with the truth of God's Word and surrender to the guiding influence of His Spirit, may we walk with confidence and conviction, knowing that our integrity is a testimony to the faithfulness and goodness of our Heavenly Father. And may our lives be a reflection of His glory, shining brightly in a world hungry for authenticity and truth.

Chapter 10:
Staying Close to God: Nurturing Our Relationship with God

In the flow of life, staying close to God is essential for nourishing and sustaining our spiritual well-being. In this chapter, we delve into the importance of cultivating intimacy with the Divine, anchored in the timeless truths of Scripture and guided by the promptings of the Holy Spirit.

Scripture offers us invaluable wisdom on how to stay close to God in our daily lives. In the book of Psalms, King David writes, "As the deer pants for streams of water, so my soul pants for you, my God. My soul thirsts for God, for the living God" (Psalm 42:1-2, NIV). This imagery captures the deep longing and desire for intimacy with God that resides within the human heart, urging us to seek His presence with fervent devotion.

One of the most effective ways to stay close to God is through regular communion with Him in prayer. In the Gospel of Luke, we read that Jesus Himself often withdrew to lonely places to pray and commune with His Heavenly Father (Luke 5:16, NIV). Following His example, we are encouraged to carve out sacred moments of solitude and silence in our own lives, where we can pour out our hearts to God in prayer and listen for His still, small voice.

Another vital aspect of staying close to God is immersing ourselves in His Word. In his second letter to Timothy, the apostle Paul writes, "All Scripture is God-breathed and is useful for teaching, rebuking, correcting and training in righteousness, so that the servant of God may be thoroughly equipped for every good work" (2 Timothy 3:16-17, NIV). By regularly studying and meditating on Scripture, we gain deeper insights into God's character and His will for our lives, drawing closer to Him in the process.

Furthermore, staying close to God involves cultivating a lifestyle of worship and gratitude. In the book of Hebrews, we're exhorted to "continually offer to God a sacrifice of praise—the fruit of lips that openly profess his name" (Hebrews 13:15, NIV). Whether through singing hymns and spiritual songs, practicing acts of kindness and generosity, or simply expressing gratitude for His blessings, we can cultivate an attitude of worship that draws us nearer to God's heart.

Ultimately, staying close to God requires intentionality, discipline, and a willingness to surrender to His leading in our lives. As we commit ourselves to prayer, study, worship, and gratitude, we open our hearts to the transformative work of the Holy Spirit, who draws us ever closer into the embrace of our Heavenly Father.

Staying close to God is not a one-time event but a lifelong journey of intimacy and communion with the Divine. As we prioritize our relationship with God above all else and seek His presence with earnestness and humility, may we experience the fullness of His love, grace, and peace that surpasses all understanding. And may our lives be a living testimony to the profound truth that in His presence, we find our truest joy and fulfillment.

31 Affirmations for Walking with God

1. Today, I choose to walk in step with God, trusting His guidance and provision for my journey.

2. I am a beloved child of God, and He walks beside me every step of the way.

3. In God's presence, I find strength, peace, and comfort for whatever challenges I may face.

4. I embrace each day as an opportunity to grow closer to God and deepen my relationship with Him.

5. I release my worries and fears into God's hands, knowing that He holds my future securely.

6. With God as my guide, I walk in confidence, knowing that His plans for me are good and full of hope.

7. I am grateful for the blessings God has bestowed upon me, and I walk in gratitude for His unfailing love.

8. When I stumble or falter, I trust in God's grace to lift me up and set me back on course.

9. I walk with humility, recognizing my need for God's wisdom and direction in every area of my life.

10. Each step I take with God brings me closer to the person He created me to be.

11. I walk with courage, knowing that God goes before me and prepares the way ahead.

12. I am filled with peace as I walk in the presence of God, knowing that He is my refuge and strength.

13. I walk with integrity, honoring God with my words, actions, and thoughts.

14. In times of uncertainty, I walk by faith, trusting that God will lead me through the storm.

15. I walk in love, extending grace and compassion to those I encounter along the way.

16. With God as my companion, I walk with purpose and passion, knowing that my life has meaning and significance.

17. I walk with perseverance, trusting that God will give me the strength to overcome every obstacle.

18. I walk with joy in my heart, rejoicing in the goodness and faithfulness of God.

19. I walk in freedom, liberated from fear and bondage by the power of God's love.

20. With each step I take, I am transformed by the renewing of my mind in Christ.

21. I walk in unity with my brothers and sisters in Christ, knowing that together, we are stronger.

22. I walk with gratitude for the beauty of God's creation, marveling at His handiwork all around me.

23. I walk with patience, trusting in God's perfect timing for every aspect of my life.

24. I walk in obedience to God's Word, knowing that His commands are for my good and His glory.

25. I walk with compassion, reaching out to those in need and sharing the love of Christ with them.

26. I walk with resilience, knowing that God will sustain me through every trial and tribulation.

27. I walk with humility, recognizing that it is God who sustains me and gives me strength.

28. I walk with gratitude for the gift of salvation and the privilege of knowing God personally.

29. I walk with boldness, knowing that God has equipped me with everything I need to fulfill His purpose for my life.

30. I walk with expectancy, anticipating the great things that God has in store for me.

31. I walk with praise on my lips and thanksgiving in my heart, for God is worthy of all honor and glory.

Final Prayer

Heavenly Father,

As I embark on this journey of walking with You, I come before Your presence with reverence and gratitude. Thank You for the privilege of knowing You and experiencing Your love in my life. Today, I commit to walking in step with You, trusting Your guidance and provision for every step of the way.

Lord, as I walk with You, I ask for Your presence to be palpable in my life. May Your Spirit guide me and lead me along paths of righteousness for Your name's sake. Help me to lean not on my own understanding but to acknowledge You in all my ways, knowing that You will direct my paths.

Father, I surrender my fears, worries, and uncertainties into Your loving hands. Strengthen my faith and grant me the courage to trust in Your unfailing promises, even when the road ahead seems uncertain. Fill me with Your peace that surpasses all understanding, guarding my heart and mind in Christ Jesus.

Teach me, Lord, to walk in integrity, honoring You with my words, actions, and thoughts. May my life be a reflection of Your love and grace, shining brightly in a world in need of Your light. Help me to walk in love, extending grace and compassion to those I encounter along the way.

Lord, I pray for wisdom and discernment as I navigate the challenges and opportunities that lie ahead. May Your Word be a lamp unto my feet and a light unto my path, illuminating the way forward and guiding me in Your truth.

Thank You, Lord, for the privilege of walking with You each day. May my journey be marked by faith, obedience, and a deepening intimacy with You. All glory, honor, and praise belong to You, now and forevermore.

In Jesus' name, I pray,

Amen.

Final Thoughts

As we bring our journey through "Walking with God" to a close, let us pause to reflect on the profound truths and transformative insights we've encountered along the way. This devotional isn't just a collection of words on a page—it's a vibrant tapestry woven with the threads of faith, hope, and love, inviting us to embark on a modern-day adventure of spiritual discovery.

In the midst of life's busyness and chaos, it's all too easy to lose sight of our connection with the Divine. Yet, as we've journeyed through these pages, we've been reminded time and again of the profound truth that God is with us every step of the way. From the depths of despair to the heights of joy, His presence is our constant companion, guiding us, comforting us, and leading us ever closer to His heart.

As we bid farewell to this devotional, let us carry with us the lessons learned and the experiences shared, allowing them to shape and transform our lives. Let us walk boldly in faith, trusting in God's guidance even when the path ahead seems uncertain. For as the psalmist declares, "Your word is a lamp for my feet, a light on my path" (Psalm 119:105, NIV). May His Word illuminate our journey and lead us to places of greater intimacy and understanding.

And so, as we venture forth into the fast-paced world that awaits us, may we do so with hearts open to the leading of the Holy Spirit. May we embrace each moment as an opportunity to draw closer to our Creator, knowing that in His presence, we find strength, peace, and joy beyond measure. And may the words of this devotional echo in our hearts as a constant reminder of the enduring truth that we are never alone, for God walks with us every step of the way. Amen.

About the Author

Rodriguez McGruder wears many hats: husband, father, and ex-FBI agent, with a background in Pentagon work. As an entrepreneur, he owns R. McGruder Handyman Services, but his true passion lies in bringing men to Christ. A budding author, he's penned his first book and eagerly anticipates writing more in the future.

Write to God

_____

_____

_____

_____

_____

_____

_____

_____

_____

_____

_____

_____

_____

_____

_____

_____

Made in the USA
Columbia, SC
07 July 2024

38180041R00030